MORMONISM AND CHRISTIANITY:

CHRISTIANITY'S ANSWERS

BY REV. JASON BIETTE

MORMONISM AND CHRISTIANITY:

CHRISTIANITY'S ANSWERS

Printed in the United States of America

First Printing, 2013

ISBN-13: 978-0615916040

ISBN-10: 061591604X

Oakwood Covenant Press
260 Oakwood Avenue
Troy, NY 12182

TABLE OF CONTENTS

Introduction

The contemporary landscape of religious sects and institutions is vast and varied. That is not to say that it is any more complex than at any other time in history, yet it may be that the level of complexity, or the blurring of evangelical distinctives, and possibly both, have made things more difficult to interpret than at times in the past. The recent uptick of Mormons and Mormonism in the news over the last several years, and the split evangelical commentary on the standing of Mormonism within the orthodox Christian compendium is a prime example which is attested to by an article in First Things in 2008 between two prominent scholars (one Mormon and one Christian) debating the Christianity of Mormonism.[1]

The purpose of this paper is to submit that Mormonism, as a form of polytheism, exists as a false theistic system.[2] This simply means that as a worldview Mormonism may be plausible, as Groothuis points out that it "holds interest and appeal for a significant number of people at a particular time and place," but when compared to the Christian worldview it is not credible.[3] To the extent that Mormonism is not credible, as a system, this paper will not only show where it fails to answer important questions, but also where Christianity truly does provide those answers.

---

[1] Bruce D. Porter, and Gerald R. McDermott. "Is Mormonism Christian?," *First Things* 186 (2008): 35-41, http://web.ebscohost.com.ezproxy.liberty.edu:2048/ehost/pdfviewer/pdfviewer?vid=11&sid=a53ab257-a1d7-4918-9caa-7c5157c38622%40sessionmgr113&hid=127 (accessed July 19, 2013).

[2] Douglas Groothuis, *Christian Apologetics: A Comprehenisve Case for Biblical Faith* (Downers Grove: InterVarsity Press, 2011), 50.

[3] Ibid.

Finally, it should be stressed that this paper is a critique of Mormonism as a system, and does not speak to the topic of the issue of individual soteriology within that system.

Individual Soteriology

A brief word about individual salvation must be written before analyzing the fundamental tenets of Mormonism. First, if it is to be posited, as is the point of this paper, that Mormonism stands outside of Christianity then all apologetic conversations with Mormons must include a presentation of the Gospel. Frame speaks specifically to this when he writes that "the apologist must always be ready to present the Gospel."[4] He explains further by showing that although the tools of apologetics are important, they should not entangle the apologist so much that he fails to share the Gospel.[5] Bahnsen also expounds

---

[4] John M. Frame, *Apologetics to the Glory of God* (Phillipsburg: P & R Publishing, 1994), 54.

[5] Ibid.

strong reasons for the apologist to view his work evangelistically.

> The apologist should declare the self-evidencing and authoritative truth of God as the precondition of intelligibility and man's only way of salvation (from all the effects of sin, including ignorance and intellectual vanity).[6]

Second, in the complexity of religion and people's belief, it may be the case that someone who holds to the Mormon worldview may also have a saving faith, albeit truncated and immature, in Jesus Christ. It is also the case that Mormons will view themselves as a part of Christianity, and in either scenario the apologist must be able to practice internal apologetics. Recognizing that this may be the case, the apologist must exercise discernment and wisdom, even as Groothuis delineates the difference between internal and external apologetics.

---

[6] Greg L. Bahnsen, *Always Ready,* ed. Robert R. Booth (Atlanta: American Vision, 1996), 80.

People are internal to Christianity if they call themselves Christian, if they self-identify with the Christian community and worldview, and people are external if they do not. Where the goal of external apologetics is to encourage a change of mind in the skeptic, the goal of *internal apologetics* is to reinforce faith, to remove intellectual barriers, to help clarify issues and in so doing dispel doubts.[7]

[7] James K. Beilby, *Thinking About Christian Apologetics: What It Is and Why We Do It* (Downers Grove: InterVarsity Press, 2011), 28.

Mormonism's Worldview

The worldview and belief system of Mormonism is extremely complex (one of the aspects which renders it untenable). Keeping this in mind, this paper will review several of the major tenets of Mormon theology. The first, according to the work of Martin, is the Mormon theology of the priesthood.

> The Mormons maintain that Joseph Smith and Oliver Cowdery received the Aaronic priesthood from the hand of John the Baptist on May 15, 1829, and that "the Melchizedek priesthood was conferred upon Joseph Smith and Oliver Cowdery through the ministration of Peter, James and John

shortly after the conferring of the Aaronic order."[8]

Martin goes on to explain that the Mormon view is that all authority comes through this united priesthood, that it is there to minister to men in all matters spiritual and physical, and that it is also broken down into a very complex hierarchical structure.[9] He concludes this section by stating: "in Mormon theology the priesthood occupies a position of great importance and comprehends every male member of the church above the age of twelve in one capacity or another."[10]

Second is the Mormon doctrine of God. Martin quotes extensively from several Mormon authoritative sources, ultimately concluding that "Mormon theology then is polytheistic, teaching in effect that the universe is inhabited by different gods who

---

[8] Walter R. Martin, *The Kingdom of the Cults*, rev. ed. (Minneapolis: Bethany Fellowship, Inc., Publishers, 1968), 171.

[9] Ibid., 172.

[10] Ibid.

procreate spirit children which are in turn clothed with bodies on different planets."[11]

Third is the Mormon teaching on the Holy Spirit. Martin quotes Talmage (a Mormon authority) and his writing.

> Talmage declares that the Holy Spirit is a personage of spirit, obviously "an immaterial being" and obviously God, and yet not possessing a form of material nature; hence, not limited to extension and space, and therefore rendering it possible for him to occupy at one time more than one space of such limits, in direct contradiction to Talmage's earlier statements in the same volume. For the Mormon then "a thing without parts has no whole and an immaterial body cannot exist," and yet the Holy Spirit is a personage of spirit."[12]

---

[11] Ibid., 179.

[12] Ibid., 184.

In this section Martin also quotes Brigham Young extensively. Martin concludes, based on Young and on the writings of various other Mormon theologians, that according to Mormonism the Spirit is "a substance, a fluid, and a person."[13]

Fourth is the Mormon doctrine of the virgin birth and here Martin again quotes Brigham Young.

> When the virgin Mary conceived the child Jesus, the father had begotten him in his own likeness. He was *not* begotten by the Holy Ghost. And who was the father? He was the first of the human family ... Jesus our elder brother was begotten in the flesh by the same character that was in the Garden of Eden and who is our father in heaven.[14]

Martin goes on to explain, based on Young's writings, that this is a reference to Adam, and therefore based

---

[13] Ibid.

[14] Ibid., 186.

18

on the polytheistic underpinnings of these teachings Adam came as one god to procreate other gods, specifically to give physical form to preexistent souls.[15]

The last tenet of the Mormon worldview and faith is the teaching on salvation and judgment. Here Martin succinctly explains that "the Mormon doctrine of salvation involves not only faith in Christ, but baptism by immersion, obedience to the teaching of the Mormon church, good works, and "keeping the commandments of God (which) will cleanse away the stain of sin.""[16] In explaining the role grace plays in the Mormon doctrine of salvation (specifically showing that it is a works based system) Martin writes that "it is they who must strive for perfection, sanctification, and godhood."[17]

Now, having established the fundamental tenets of Mormonism, much of which is based on the

---

[15] Ibid.

[16] Ibid., 190.

[17] Ibid., 194

writings and teachings of the founders of the religion, it is beneficial to analyze more contemporary Mormon writing and literature to evaluate whether or not any adjustments have been made in recent years to Mormon theology. This is especially appropriate as it has been shown that in the very recent past Mormonism has been posited by both Mormons and Christians alike as just another sect within evangelical Christianity.

An example of this is Mason, who while analyzing the early beliefs of Mormonism in relation to state perpetrated violence writes that "the Doctrine and Covenants was and is authoritative for Latter-Day Saints; it is concise; it is prescriptive rather than descriptive; and its historical setting is basically modern."[18] This is imminently important to the discussion at hand; first, in recognition that the

---

[18] Patrick Q. Mason. ""The Wars and the Perplexities of the Nations": Reflections on Early Mormonism, Violence, and the State," *Journal of Mormon History* 38, no. 3 (2012): 77, http://web.ebscohost.com.ezproxy.liberty.edu:2048/ehost/pdfviewer/pdfviewer?sid=06c3895d-64d0-43b1-97d5-ce7018faa308%40sessionmgr198&vid=4&hid=122 (accessed August 12, 2013).

Doctrine and Covenants is one of the authorities of Mormon doctrine, and second, in the affirmation of its authority even today. Much of what Martin writes about Mormonism comes directly from the Doctrine and Covenants. Another example of this is found in a paper written by Park. The position of the paper is to critique previous analysis of early Mormon history, which generally tries to show that early Mormon thought borrowed or stole its ideas from contemporary philosophies and theologies. It is Park's concluding thought which speaks to the question of Mormon worldview in recent history.

> For the next generation of LDS scholarship, those who wish to explore Mormonism's developing theology must first understand the intellectual air which its early adherents breathed, recognizing the eclectic theological climate of varying degrees of adaptation and agreement, and then attempt to determine the significance of Mormonism's mesh of

theological answers. And, once these answers are better understood, it is then crucial to apply them to larger cultural questions and issues, emphasizing how Mormonism related to and diverged from their larger environment. Indeed, one of the great achievements of the New Mormon History was using broader contexts to better illuminate early Mormon thought. Now it is time to use early Mormon thought to further illuminate its broader contexts.[19]

The point that Park makes, which is relevant to the purpose of this paper, is that early Mormon

---

[19] Benjamin E. Park. "Reasonings Sufficient": Joseph Smith, Thomas Dick, and the Context(s) of Early Mormonism," *Journal of Mormon History* 38, no. 3 (2012): 223-224, http://web.ebscohost.com.ezproxy.liberty.edu:2048/ehost/pdfviewer/pdfviewer?sid=50ffdece-670d-4583-9717-d4b564828cde%40sessionmgr115&vid=4&hid=122 (accessed August 13, 2013).

thought should be viewed as the standard by which contextual study; historical, philosophical, and theological, of that time period is analyzed through, thus once again in the modern era establishing the worldview and system of Mormonism as not only correct, but ultimate.

In the final analysis, research shows and establishes not only what the major tenets of Mormon theology are, as originally established by the founders during its formative years, but also, even more importantly, recent Mormon scholarship exemplifies a continued adherence to those writings; their doctrines and theologies, as authoritative.

Mormon Lifestyle

One of the challenges of the current debate is found in the life that the typical Mormon leads. In the eyes of the uninitiated, Mormons lead "good Christian lives." They are generally regarded, within the culture, as moral and ethical individuals, family-oriented, and socially and fiscally conservative. There is then obvious parallel with the societal platforms which most evangelical Christians hold, and it is understandable that Mormons, Christians and the non-religious alike easily view Mormons as just a small part of the larger evangelical milieu.

> The average Mormon is usually marked by many sound moral traits. He is generally amiable, almost always hospitable, and extremely devoted to

his family and to the teachings of his church.[20]

Martin goes on to explain that although this is often the case, it is also often the case that the individual Mormon knows very little of the historical background of the teachings of Mormonism, which is ultimately by design.[21]

It should also be noted that the orthodox and historical teachings of Christianity do not generally state that being a good moral and ethical conservative family-man makes one a Christian. The Mormon lifestyle may be a commendable one, but it is not necessarily a Christian one.

[20] Walter R. Martin, *The Kingdom of the Cults*, rev. ed. (Minneapolis: Bethany Fellowship, Inc., Publishers, 1968), 149.

[21] Ibid., 149-150.

An Evaluation of the Mormon Worldview

The recognition that the worldview of Mormonism is complex does not necessitate a complex evaluation. Groothuis delineates eight criteria for evaluating a worldview, many of which become self-evident when analyzing the worldview at hand.[22] For example, it has already been noted that the complexity of Mormonism's worldview makes it ultimately an untenable one. Groothuis explains that no two propositions can contradict themselves in his second criterion.[23] The above discussion of Mormonism's teachings on the Holy Spirit clearly falls

---

[22] Douglas Groothuis, *Christian Apologetics: A Comprehenisve Case for Biblical Faith* (Downers Grove: InterVarsity Press, 2011), 53-60.

[23] Ibid., 53.

under this second criterion. Another example is Groothuis' seventh criterion which states that "if a worldview substantially alters its essential claims in light of counterevidence, it loses rational justification."[24] Martin speaks to this issue as well when he writes that "from the foregoing, which are only a handful of examples of the more than two thousand changes to be found in the *Book of Mormon* over a period of 131 years, the reader can see that it is in no sense to be accepted as the Word of God."[25] Martin, in recording the history of Mormonism also gives evidence which fits into Groothuis' fourth criterion in which he writes that a worldview is more likely to be true when its essential propositions are empirically verifiable both scientifically and historically.[26] He extensively details specific examples

---

[24] Ibid., 58.

[25] Walter R. Martin, *The Kingdom of the Cults*, rev. ed. (Minneapolis: Bethany Fellowship, Inc., Publishers, 1968), 164.

[26] Douglas Groothuis, *Christian Apologetics: A Comprehenisve Case for Biblical Faith* (Downers Grove: InterVarsity Press, 2011), 55.

of scientific and archaeological evidences against the authenticity of the Book of Mormon.[27] A final example can be made of Groothuis' eighth criterion in which he writes that "worldviews should not appeal to extraneous entities or be more complex than is required to explain what they propose to establish."[28] This is certainly true regarding the Book of Mormon.

> According to the Mormons, the *Book of Mormon* is a condensation of the high points of these ancient civilizations. The author of the book is a prophet named Mormon. The book is "the translation of the abridgment of the record of these civilizations" and "includes a brief outline of the history of the earlier

---

[27] Walter R. Martin, *The Kingdom of the Cults*, rev. ed. (Minneapolis: Bethany Fellowship, Inc., Publishers, 1968), 159-163.

[28] Douglas Groothuis, *Christian Apologetics: A Comprehenisve Case for Biblical Faith* (Downers Grove: InterVarsity Press, 2011), 59.

Jaredite people, an abridgement made by Moroni, son of Mormon, taken from Jaredite record found during the period of the second civilization."[29]

When all of this evidence is taken in the whole, what is shown to be the case is that the worldview of Mormonism is founded on the unverifiable testimony of one man, receiving complex prophecy in written and verbal form from sources which are unverifiable historically and scientifically and which, as the course of time progresses, has been changed on thousands of occasions to explain away contradictions. Based on just these few and simple criteria it is highly unlikely that Mormonism presents a credible worldview.

One final note is sufficient in this section. Although it is now becoming increasingly clear that Mormonism is a worldview which is completely unsustainable, namely because of what has been written above, that work may not suffice to show

---

[29] Walter R. Martin, *The Kingdom of the Cults*, rev. ed. (Minneapolis: Bethany Fellowship, Inc., Publishers, 1968), 157.

(especially to those who are unfamiliar) that it is all that different from Christianity. Bernard Ramm, in the introduction to a paper studying the apologetics of the Old Testament unwittingly clears up this challenge.

> The New Testament presumes the existence of God and certain of his attributes, the doctrine of creation and the associated doctrines of preservation and providence, the existence and supreme worth of the spiritual order, and, the concept of God's purposes at work in human history bringing to pass the will of God, especially in the realms of judgment and salvation. Although it is true that Christianity makes certain significant additions to these doctrines and presumptions, it nevertheless seems obvious to me that the basic theistic scheme here so briefly outlined is carried over from the Old

31

Testament by the writers of the New Testament.[30]

If what Ramm writes is to be taken as an accurate summary of the Christian worldview, which this paper does, then it is obvious that the worldview of Mormonism and the worldview of Christianity are incompatible.

---

[30] Bernard L. Ramm, "The Apologetic of the Old Testament: The Basis of a Biblical and Christian Apologetic," *Bulletin of the Evangelical Theological Society* 1, no. 4 (1958): 15, http://web.ebscohost.com.ezproxy.liberty.edu:2048/ehost/pdfviewer/pdfviewer?sid=b5664367-dbaf-4cdb-acf2-7bb44eb03733%40sessionmgr104&vid=13&hid=122 (accessed August 14, 2013).

Christianity's Response

Establishing Christianity's answer to Mormonism begins with establishing Christianity's truth as the replacement for the false truth presented by Mormonism, and establishing that truth based on the Bible. Whitcomb writes

> The biblical method of winning men to Christ (including present-day intellectuals) is to present the true gospel lovingly, patiently, and prayerfully "according to the Scriptures" (1 Cor. 15:3) from the context of a godly life (1 Thess. 1:5; 2:3-12). Only the "living and powerful" Word of God can permeate the unbeliever's shield of defense and

pierce into his heart (Heb. 4:12), and thus only God may receive the glory for the genuine conversion of sinful men[31]

To begin, it has been shown that Mormonism, at its core, is a polytheistic worldview, which means, by extension, that although the divinity of Jesus may not be called into question, the uniqueness of His divinity certainly is. The fundamental answer that Christianity brings before the Mormon worldview specifically speaks to that question; namely that Jesus as God incarnate is uniquely divine, uniquely the Son of God. This sets Him apart from the rest of humanity, ultimately transcendent, although His transcendence does not set Him so apart from mankind that He is unreachable. Groothuis speaks to this very topic when he writes

---

[31] John C. Whitcomb Jr, "Contemporary Apologetics and the Christian Faith Part II: Christian Apologetics and the Dive Solution," *Bibliotheca Sacra* 134, no. 535 (1977): 196, http://web.ebscohost.com.ezproxy.liberty.edu:2048/ehost/pdfviewer/pdfviewer?sid=b5664367-dbaf-4cdb-acf2-7bb44eb03733%40sessionmgr104&vid=8&hid=122 (accessed August 14, 2013).

... the cumulative evidence singles Jesus out from all other religious figures. He entered the world supernaturally, accredited himself with unparalleled signs and wonders, possessed an impeccable character, made claims only befitting God himself, and died with the purpose of redeeming humanity. The best account of the historical facts is that he was who he said he was. If this is so, we should respond to him on his terms.[32]

The importance of the uniqueness of who Jesus was and what he did cannot be understated. Mormonism posits that there are many gods and that humanity and divinity are intertwined, and therefore, as has been shown, there is no clear and distinct path within the belief system to salvation. The individual

---

[32] Douglas Groothuis, *Christian Apologetics: A Comprehenisve Case for Biblical Faith* (Downers Grove: InterVarsity Press, 2011), 503.

must "do the right things" and do them in the right way in order to be saved. Jesus, ultimately, is no different than any other god-man, and in some cases is presented as much less. Martin explains

> The Saviour of Mormonism, however, is an entirely different person, as their official publications clearly reveal. The Mormon Saviour is not the second person of the Christian Trinity since, as we have seen previously, Mormons reject the Christian doctrine of the Trinity and he is not even a careful replica of the New Testament redeemer. In Mormon theology, Christ as a pre-existent spirit was not only the brother of the devil (*Pearl of Great* Price, Book of Moses, Chapter 4, Verses 1-4) but celebrated his own marriage to "both the Marys and to Martha, whereby he could see his seed before he was crucified." As we have seen

previously the Mormon concept of the virgin birth, alone, distinguishes their "Christ" from the Christ of the Bible.

In addition to this revolting concept, Brigham Young categorically stated that the sacrifice made upon the cross by Jesus Christ in the form of His own blood was ineffective for the cleansing of *some* sins.[33]

These teachings stand in very sharp contrast to the teachings of biblical Christianity. The unique divinity of Jesus Christ should be viewed as not only the cornerstone of the Christian belief system, but also as *the* blow against the credibility of Mormonism, even as Groothuis sums up when he writes that "when carefully stated and explained, the idea of the incarnation is shown to be logically coherent, awe-inspiring, unique and wonderful for errant mortals in

---

[33] Walter R. Martin, *The Kingdom of the Cults*, rev. ed. (Minneapolis: Bethany Fellowship, Inc., Publishers, 1968), 192.

need of divine rescue."[34]   There is no Christianity without Christ, ultimately because there is no salvation without Christ, and that is the answer that Mormonism needs.

[34] Douglas Groothuis, *Christian Apologetics: A Comprehenisve Case for Biblical Faith* (Downers Grove: InterVarsity Press, 2011), 503.

A Planned Defense

The first step in developing a plan to defend Christianity to the Mormon must follow from the above discussion of Christianity's answer to Mormonism, namely the unique divinity of Jesus Christ. When one upholds the doctrine of Jesus Christ's divinity then what necessarily follows is the understanding that the resurrection of Christ is absolutely essential. This, then, can be used as a foil to show that in the Mormon worldview, Christ's resurrection must not be all that important. In the Mormon worldview, He exists just as one god of many, which negates the efficacious atoning nature of His sacrifice. The resurrection of Jesus is Christian evidence, and as Whitcomb points out in the following quote it can be a powerful and useful tool.

If used "lawfully," however, Christian evidences can have great value. For the *believer*, they can provide a certain degree of intellectual satisfaction, deeper appreciation for the marvels and complexities of God's universe, and helpful background materials for the study of various aspects of biblical revelation. For the *unbeliever*, they can be used to arouse interest and hold attention (somewhat like the sign-miracles during the period of the Gospels and the Book of Acts), if carefully and skillfully handled by the Christian *in conjunction with a true Gospel witness*.[35]

---

[35] John C.Whitcomb Jr, "Contemporary Apologetics and the Christian Faith Part IV: The Limitations and Values of Christian Evidences, " *Bibliotheca Sacra* 135, no. 537 (1978): 31, http://web.ebscohost.com.ezproxy.liberty.edu:2048/ehost/pdfviewer/pdfviewer?sid=a53ab257-a1d7-4918-9caa-7c5157c38622%40sessionmgr113&vid=6&hid=127 (accessed August 15, 2013).

With this being said, the resurrection needs to be defended as the central Christian evidence, as Groothuis points out that "the resurrection of Jesus is at the center of the Christian worldview and Christian devotion.[36] Standing in sharp contrast to the worldview of Mormonism, a very strong and simple case can be formulated for the veracity of the resurrection of Jesus. In summary, the historically verifiable evidences are; Jesus was crucified by the Roman method of crucifixion and this leaves no question as to whether or not He was truly dead, the tomb that He was buried in is known and verifiable as well as the fact that the tomb was then empty, and Jesus appeared numerous times after His death and these appearances are attested to by many, sometimes numerous eyewitness accounts.[37] Groothuis then provides further argumentation, which again stands in sharp contrast to Mormonism, as the fact that the

---

[36] Douglas Groothuis, *Christian Apologetics: A Comprehenisve Case for Biblical Faith* (Downers Grove: InterVarsity Press, 2011), 528.

[37] Ibid., 540-546.

disciples were transformed to "those who had beheld the risen Christ and who, on that basis, preached Him as the Lord of life and the judge of history."[38] The disciples, simply put, became people who were willing to sacrifice everything, including their own lives, based on the fact that Jesus had indeed resurrected.

A second point of discussion with Mormonism is found in the so called problem of evil. The Mormon worldview posits no solution to this problem. Groothuis defines the problem of evil thusly, "Simply put, if God exists, there should not be such evil, since God would have the power and desire to stop it. Therefore, the existence or goodness or power of God is brought into question."[39] The Mormon worldview has a very interesting way of dealing with this. Paulsen, in the *Encyclopedia of Mormonism* explains in the entry on evil.

---

[38] Ibid., 551.

[39] Douglas Groothuis, *Christian Apologetics: A Comprehenisve Case for Biblical Faith* (Downers Grove: InterVarsity Press, 2011), 614-615.

Latter-day Saints reject the troublesome premise of creation ex nihilo (out of nothing), affirming rather that there are actualities that are coeternal with God. These coeternal actualities include INTELLIGENCES (sometimes perceived as primal selves or persons), chaotic matter (or mass energy), and laws and principles (perhaps best regarded as the properties and relations of matter and intelligences). Given this plurality of uncreated entities, it does not follow, within an LDS worldview, that God is the ultimate source of evil. Evil is traceable, alternatively, to the choices of other autonomous agents (such as Lucifer, the Devil) who are also coeternal with God, and, perhaps, even to recalcitrant properties of uncreated chaotic matter.[40]

---

[40] David L. Paulsen, "Evil," in *Encyclopedia of*

What this means, beside the fact that there are entities that have existed coeternally with God, is that although God was never the source of evil, evil has existed along with God coeternally. This therefore means that evil preexisted the fall, and therefore this changes all understanding of the atonement. In one sense the Mormon worldview posits that there is no problem with evil because it has always existed, even outside of God. The conundrum that this creates is that there is no need to do anything with, or do anything about evil. Evil is not something to ultimately be conquered, but it is something to always be endured. Again, what is seen is that the answer to this is found in the warp and woof of Christianity. The fundamental answer of Christianity is the unique divinity of Jesus Christ, which flows to the first defense, namely the resurrection of Jesus Christ, which then informs the problem of evil, ignored by Mormonism, but dealt with head on with Christianity, even as Groothuis

Mormonism, ed. Daniel H. Ludlow (New York: Macmillan Publishing Company, 1992), 478.

points out that "the single greatest example of good triumphing over evil is the death of Jesus Christ on a cross outside of ancient Jerusalem."[41] He goes on to show that no other worldview, including Mormonism

> ... teaches that God Almighty humbled himself in order to redeem his sinful creatures through his own suffering and death. No other worldview endorses the idea that the supreme reality was impaled by human hands for the sake of lost souls. No founder of any other religion cried out in his sacrificial death, "My God, my God, why have you forsaken me?" (Matthew 27:46; see Psalm 22:1)[42]

---

[41] Douglas Groothuis, *Christian Apologetics: A Comprehenisve Case for Biblical Faith* (Downers Grove: InterVarsity Press, 2011), 644.

[42] Ibid.

Conclusion

This paper clearly shows that Mormonism stands, in no uncertain terms, outside of Christian orthodoxy. Based on the fundamentals of the Mormon worldview, it should never be considered as just another corner of evangelical Christianity. Further, far from standing outside of Christianity, Mormonism does not even stand up as a credible worldview on its own. It is too complex to be considered logical or rational, and it is contradictory in just about all of its aspects. On top of all this, the sources of Mormonism, verbal and written testimony are completely unverifiable.

Christianity not only provides the only viable answer to Mormonism, it provides the only true answer for mankind, which is found in the person and work of Jesus Christ. Therefore, although a fairly simple and straightforward apologetic against Mormonism can be formed from the tenets of the Christian faith, that apologetic should always be delivered as a part of the Gospel message.

Bibliography

Bahnsen, Greg L. *Always Ready*. Edited. by Robert R. Booth. Atlanta: American Vision, 1996.

Beilby, James K. *Thinking About Christian Apologetics: What It Is and Why We Do It*. Downers Grove: InterVarsity Press, 2011.

Groothuis, Douglas. *Christian Apologetics: A Comprehenisve Case for Biblical Faith*. Downers Grove: InterVarsity Press, 2011.

Martin, Walter R. *The Kingdom of the Cults*. rev. ed. Minneapolis: Bethany Fellowship, Inc., Publishers, 1968.

Mason, Patrick Q. ""The Wars and the Perplexities of the Nations": Reflections on Early Mormonism, Violence, and the State." *Journal of Mormon History* 38, no. 3 (2012). http://web.ebscohost.com.ezproxy.liberty.edu:2048/ehost/pdfviewer/pdfviewer?sid=06c3895d-64d0-43b1-97d5-

ce7018faa308%40sessionmgr198&vid=4&hid=122 (accessed August 12, 2013).

Park, Benjamin E. ""Reasonings Sufficient": Joseph Smith, Thomas Dick, and the Context(s) of Early Mormonism." *Journal of Mormon History* 38, no. 3 (2012). http://web.ebscohost.com.ezproxy.liberty.edu:2048/eh ost/pdfviewer/pdfviewer?sid=50ffdece-670d-4583-9717-d4b564828cde%40sessionmgr115&vid=4&hid=122 (accessed August 13, 2013).

Paulsen, David L. "Evil." In *Encyclopedia of Mormonism*, edited by Daniel H. Ludlow, 477-478. New York: Macmillan Publishing Company, 1992.

Porter, Bruce D. and Gerald R. McDermott. "Is Mormonism Christian." *First Things* 186 (2008). http://web.ebscohost.com.ezproxy.liberty.edu:2048/eh ost/pdfviewer/pdfviewer?vid=11&sid=a53ab257-a1d7-4918-9caa-7c5157c38622%40sessionmgr113&hid=127 (accessed July 19, 2013).

Ramm, Bernard L. "The Apologetic of the Old Testament: The Basis of a Biblical and Christian Apologetic." *Bulletin of the Evangelical Theological Society* 1, no. 4 (1958). http://web.ebscohost.com.ezproxy.liberty.edu:2048/eh

ost/pdfviewer/pdfviewer?sid=b5664367-dbaf-4cdb-
acf2-
7bb44eb03733%40sessionmgr104&vid=13&hid=122
(accessed August 14, 2013).

Whitcomb Jr, John C. "Contemporary Apologetics and the
Christian Faith Part II: Christian Apologetics and the
Dive Solution." *Bibliotheca Sacra* 134, no. 535 (1977).
http://web.ebscohost.com.ezproxy.liberty.edu:2048/eh
ost/pdfviewer/pdfviewer?sid=b5664367-dbaf-4cdb-
acf2-
7bb44eb03733%40sessionmgr104&vid=8&hid=122
(accessed August 14, 2013).

———. "Contemporary Apologetics and the Christian Faith
Part IV: The Limitations and Values of Christian
Evidences. " *Bibliotheca Sacra* 135, no. 537 (1978).
http://web.ebscohost.com.ezproxy.liberty.edu:2048/eh
ost/pdfviewer/pdfviewer?sid=a53ab257-a1d7-4918-
9caa-
7c5157c38622%40sessionmgr113&vid=6&hid=127 (
accessed August 15, 2013). Frame, John M. *Apologetics
to the Glory of God*. Phillipsburg: P & R Publishing, 1994.

www.ingramcontent.com/pod-product-compliance
Lightning Source LLC
Chambersburg PA
CBHW071742020426
42331CB00008B/2140